W9-BPM-555

The Skateboarder's Guide to
Skate Parks, Half-Pipes, Bowls, and Obstacles™

OFF THE WALL

A Skateboarder's Guide to Riding Bowls and Pools

Justin Hocking

The Rosen Publishing Group, Inc., New York

For Matt and Sean

Published in 2005 by The Rosen Publishing Group, Inc.
29 East 21st Street, New York, NY 10010

First Edition

Library of Congress Cataloging-in-Publication Data

Hocking, Justin.
Off the wall: a skateboarder's guide to riding bowls and pools/by Justin Hocking.— 1st ed.
    p. cm.—(The skateboarder's guide to skate parks, half-pipes, bowls, and obstacles)
Includes bibliographical references and index.
ISBN 1-4042-0339-7 (library binding)
1. Skateboarding—Juvenile literature.
I. Title. II. Series: Hocking, Justin. Skateboarder's guide to skate parks, half-pipes, bowls, and other obstacles.
GV859.8.H613 2005
796.22–dc22

                                                2004006816

Manufactured in the United States of America

On the cover: A skateboarder does a grind in a bowl.

CONTENTS

INTRODUCTION

Hey, skaters! Maybe you've already read our book *Rippin' Ramps: A Skateboarder's Guide to Riding Half-Pipes*, and now that you're comfortable skating on ramps, you're ready for a different kind of challenge.

In case you don't know, a bowl is a kind of ramp with rounded curves (also called transitions) all the way around, like a giant cereal bowl. People have been skating in bowls and empty pools, which are similar to bowls, for decades. And lately, this type of skating is increasing in popularity again.

Many skate parks feature bowls as well as ramps and obstacles. Learning how to skate bowls is an important step in becoming a first-class skater.

The fun thing about bowls and pools is that you can do a number of tricks in them that you can't do on a half-pipe. On a half-pipe, you can only skate up and down the ramp. In a bowl or a pool, though, you can skate around in one continuous motion in all directions. Needless to say, you can do a variety of cool tricks such as carves and grinds, which we'll show you how to do.

If you're a younger skater, chances are you've seen pictures or videos of people skating pools but probably have never set foot in one. Or maybe you've already skated a bowl or a pool and you want to learn some more advanced tricks. As long as you have some basic ramp skating skills down and you have access to a skateboard bowl or pool, this book is for you. We'll start out with some bowl skating basics, and then launch into some harder moves, including grinds, airs, and hip transfers, which we'll explain later.

No matter what level you're at, learning to skate bowls and pools is a lot of fun, and it will help you become a more well-rounded skater. So grab your board and get ready to skate it up!

CHAPTER 1

The Curvy World of Bowls and Pools

Imagine for a moment that you have a time machine that can transport you back to the year 1956. Believe it or not, people were skateboarding fifty years ago. But back in the 1950s, skateboarding didn't look anything like it does today.

As you step out of your time machine, you might see a group of kids rolling down the street barefoot, making slalom turns on planks of wood with rollerskate wheels nailed to the bottom. They're moving pretty slowly, and with metal wheels, they take a slam, or fall, every time they hit even the smallest pebble.

Back then, skateboarding was mainly a form of transportation, and the only tricks were things like rolling handstands, high jumps, and hang tens, where the skater rides with both feet on the nose and all ten toes hanging off the front of the board. If you asked one of these skaters to do a modern trick such as an ollie (a trick where you press down on the tail and pop your board and body up into the air), they'd have no idea what you were talking about. Boards were flat back then, and the angled kicktail that you find on the back of almost all modern skateboards hadn't even been invented.

The Beginning of Pool Skating

If you transported yourself ten years ahead from then to the 1960s, you might witness something that changed the face of skateboarding forever. At some point (no one knows exactly when), some young skateboarders discovered an empty backyard swimming pool and got an idea. You can imagine what it was like to step down out of the regular, horizontal world of the street with all its straight lines and square houses into the vertical world of an empty swimming pool, with its smoothly rounded transitions and curves. You can also imagine how much courage it took to be the first person to roll into the deep end, barefoot, on a 6-inch-wide (15.2-centimeter wide) plank with clay wheels. No one knows who this first person to skate in a pool was, but the first pool sessions can be traced as far back as 1963, to legendary skater Gary Swanson's backyard pool.

Pool riding took off in the late 1960s and 1970s, aided by the introduction of wheels made from urethane, which is a type of plastic. Urethane wheels allow skateboarders to roll much faster and smoother than clay or metal wheels do. Skaters in places such as Venice Beach (also known as Dogtown), in California, brought many of surfing's aggressive, flowing moves to pool skating. Instead of just doing handstands and other gymnastic tricks on flat sidewalks, these skaters understood that skating a pool was like riding a giant concrete wave. Legendary skaters such as Tony Alva and Jay Adams were doing what seemed impossible a few years earlier: grinding and catching airs in backyard pools. These skaters helped change a freestyle-oriented, acrobatic fad into a more aggressive, surf-style pursuit.

7

The Difference Between Pools and Bowls

Pools and bowls are basically the same thing. However, the term "pool" is usually used to describe actual backyard swimming pools that weren't originally built for skateboarding, exactly like the ones we just talked about.

Backyard pools can be a lot of fun, but they have several drawbacks, too. First of all, the chances of actually finding a backyard pool that you can skate in are pretty slim, especially if you don't live in a place with a warm climate like Southern California, Arizona, or Florida. And if you do happen to find one, it might be on private property. Also, since their transitions are usually extremely steep, backyard pools are among the most difficult of all skate terrains.

Fortunately, you can now find concrete or wooden bowls at many skate parks around the country. They're not unlike the empty swimming pools that skaters first started riding in. In fact some bowls, like the one at the Donald Skatepark in Oregon, are exact replicas of swimming pools.

However, most skate park pools have much more mellow transitions, making them the ideal setting for you to learn basic bowl skills. The tricks in this book will be illustrated mostly in wooden bowls and skate park pools. This is where we recommend you start out, the same way a novice mountain climber begins climbing a peak with a gentle slope, gradually working his or her way up to steeper faces.

Parts of a Bowl

Before you start skating in a bowl, you need to know the names of all the different elements of the bowl environment. First of all, many bowls and pools are made out of concrete. Concrete is the material of choice for a lot of reasons: it never wears out, it allows skaters to ride fast, and it can be shaped into all sorts of cool curves and forms.

This is an example of a concrete bowl with a unique shape. The split-level design, with a shallow end and a deep end, also makes this bowl more fun to ride.

One downfall of concrete is that it's rock-hard. Nothing hurts worse than a hard slam on concrete. Although slamming in a bowl never feels good, no matter what surface you land on, wooden bowls tend to give, or flex, just a little when you slam, which makes it a little less painful. However, wooden bowls are hard to build. It's a huge challenge to make concave curves using wood. But there are plenty of them out there, and they're usually surfaced with materials such as masonite, birch plywood, or the weather-resistant Skatelite.

The transitions, also called trannys or walls, are the curving sections of the bowl or pool, the parts that look like the vertical face of a

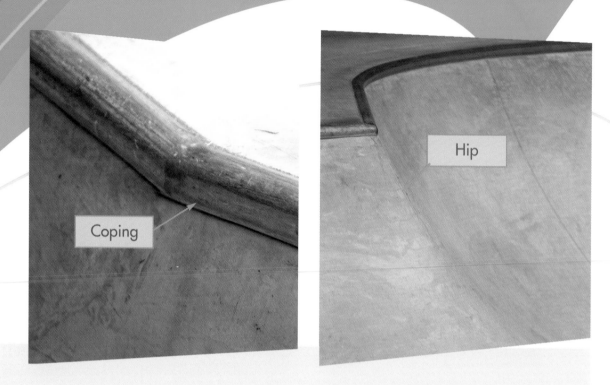

Left: The metal coping on this bowl allows skaters to do grinds and slides. Right: This is a closeup of a hip. Hips are a good place to do airs in a bowl.

frozen wave. The corners are the curving sections that connect the transitions. These are what give the bowl its rounded, cereal bowl shape. Many bowls are shaped this way, but most modern bowls have more unique shapes with at least a few "flat" walls, or straight sections to break up the corners and allow for more complex and interesting lines.

Another common bowl feature is a hip, which is where two transitions meet at an angle and jut out like an actual hip. A pool with a single hip is often called a kidney pool because it resembles the shape of a kidney.

The flat-bottom is the flat, ground-level section of the bowl that separates the transitions. Most bowls have at least ten feet (three meters) of flat-bottom, making it easier to set up for your next trick because it gives you time until you reach the opposite transition. But many backyard pools have little or no flat-bottom, which means you have to be quick on your feet.

At the top of each transition is a round metal pipe known as the coping or the lip. The coping is a surface for doing grinds and stalls, and bouncing your wheels off the coping helps you pop up above the bowl on aerial tricks.

Many backyard pools have concrete coping on the top, just above a row of ornamental tiles. Also known as pool coping, it's a much rougher surface than metal coping, and it often has lots of cracks and seams. It takes more speed and power to grind concrete coping because of its rough surface, but that's exactly what many pool skaters love about it, along with the loud "barking" sound of metal trucks grinding on concrete.

Finally, sitting on top of each transition you'll find the decks. Like the deck of a ship, this is where skaters stand before taking their next "plunge" into the pool or bowl.

CHAPTER 2

The Fundamentals: Safety, Knee Slides, and Carving

So now you know some of the history of pool skating and all the different parts of a bowl. So you're ready to get in there and rip, right? Well, hang on just a minute. You need to know that bowl and pool skating can be pretty dangerous, especially if you're not well prepared. The best way to keep yourself safe is this: always wear pads and a helmet! There are no ifs, ands, or buts about it. You have to protect yourself with skateboard-specific knee pads (sorry, but thin soccer knee pads and elbow pads won't cut it).

Companies such as Rector, Protec, and Boneless all make top-of-the-line pads, the kind with a thick plastic cap. If you've ever seen people skate a half-pipe or bowl, then you know exactly what this cap is for: after bailing a trick, instead of flopping like a dead fish to the flat-bottom, experienced skaters drop to their knees,

The most important thing to do before skating any bowl is to gear up in the proper padding. The various types of protective gear include knee pads *(bottom left)* and elbow pads *(top)*. Since falling on a half-pipe involves sliding down the transition on your knees, and sometimes on your elbows, you'll be glad that you have these pads. The most important protective gear you can wear, though, is your helmet *(bottom right)*.

and sometimes elbows, too, and slide gracefully down the transition on their pads. Before you start actually skating a half-pipe, it's a good idea to practice some knee slides without your skateboard.

Knee Slide

When you first try the knee slide, start up low on the transition. As you get the hang of it, make your way up higher. Then, after you learn to carve, which we'll cover later, try dropping off your skateboard into a knee slide.

13

KNEE SLIDE

1 Run a few feet up the transition.

2 As you near the top of the bowl, turn and jump to your knees.

3 Slide down the transition on your knee pads (never do this without pads) with your feet dragging beneath you. Place some weight on your feet but avoid sitting down too hard on your heels, which could lead to an ankle or foot injury.

4 As you slide, lean back a little. If you start to fall forward, instead of putting your hands out in front of you and risking an arm or wrist injury, fall onto your elbow pads and use them to slide, the same way you slide on your knee pads.

Once you actually start skating the bowl, it'll take a little practice to get in the habit of dropping to your knees when you take a fall. Learning to knee slide will definitely help keep you safe, but it's not a 100 percent guarantee against injury.

The truth is, if you're a skateboarder, you'll bang yourself up a little at some point. It comes with the territory, but the best way to protect yourself against serious injuries is to use your head and skate smart. It's good to push yourself and take risks, but the most important thing is to be smart and progress at your own pace. Attempting a trick that you're not ready for or trying to show off are two of the main reasons people get hurt in bowls or pools. Remember, skateboarding is not a competitive sport. You don't have to worry about trying to prove yourself to anyone. So skate smart, because it's really all about just having fun with your friends.

Whenever you show up to a bowl or pool, especially one you've never skated before, there's another important way you need to use your head—and your eyes. If there are people already skating, sit down and just watch them for a while. Pay attention to how they skate, where they drop in, and what type of lines they take. That way, once you start skating, you'll have a better understanding of the bowl itself, and you can avoid getting in anyone's way. Along with watching what kind of lines other skaters take, it's important to pay attention to the order that skaters go in. It's OK to jump into a session, but make sure to wait your turn before you take your next run.

Carving Backside

The thing that makes skating bowls fun is that, unlike on a half-pipe where you just go back and forth, you can do what's called carving. Carving allows you to move in circular patterns around the bowl, using the corners to gain momentum and speed. Once you learn how to do it, you'll find that the cool thing about carving is that it allows you to go fast and, if you want to, really fast. In fact, some people enjoy simply carving in a bowl without really doing many tricks at all.

Before you learn to carve, you should definitely be comfortable with pumping, dropping in, and doing kick turns on a half-pipe. If you don't already have these skills wired, it's a good idea at this point to go back and read our book *Rippin' Ramps: A Skateboarder's Guide to Riding Half-Pipes.*

When you skate a ramp, you maintain speed by using your legs to apply downward force on the skateboard as you move up and down each transition. This is called pumping. Many of the same pumping motions help you keep your speed in a bowl, too. But carving through a corner is just a little different than pumping on a half-pipe. Think of the corner itself as a half-pipe turned on its side. As you move through it, even though you're up on the wall, you have to pump, just like you would on a regular ramp.

Before you try carving, it's usually a good idea to grab a skate key or a wrench and loosen your trucks up a bit, especially if you normally ride with very tight trucks. Use your skate key or wrench to turn your large truck bolt (also called a kingpin) counterclockwise a few spins. This makes it easier to skate a bowl because it allows you to make sharper turns simply by leaning on your toes or heels. And before you try the next five steps, try doing a few basic kick turns in the bowl, just to warm up.

Here's a step-by-step approach to carving backside (which means you turn toward the direction of your toes):

Approach the corner backside with your knees bent slightly. Don't ride straight into the corner. Instead, approach it at a very wide, arching angle.

1

CARVING BACKSIDE

2 Your front foot should be directly above the mounting bolts for your front truck, while your back foot should rest in the spot where your tail starts to angle up. Since you're carving backside, press down slightly on the edge of your board with your toes and the balls of your feet.

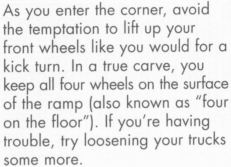

3 As you enter the corner, avoid the temptation to lift up your front wheels like you would for a kick turn. In a true carve, you keep all four wheels on the surface of the ramp (also known as "four on the floor"). If you're having trouble, try loosening your trucks some more.

4 Lean forward and stay pretty low. The more downward pressure you apply with your feet and legs, the faster you'll move through the corner.

5 Don't try to come straight down from the corner. Instead, angle down off the face wall, pumping the transition as you come down.

Carving Frontside

It's important that you learn how to carve in both directions. Carving frontside (which means you turn toward your heels) through a corner involves pretty much the same motion as a backside carve. There are a few important differences, though.

CARVING FRONTSIDE

1 Approach the wall frontside, with your knees bent and your legs slightly bowed out. When you're first learning to carve frontside, you really have to work to get your knees bent, so it's OK if you squat a little.

2 It's a little harder to see where you're going when you carve frontside, so make sure to look over your lead shoulder as you turn.

3 As you enter the corner, avoid the temptation to lean toward the coping. In order to really carve and gain speed, you have to lean back a little toward the bowl as you use all the power in your feet and legs to press down on the skateboard and pump through the corner.

4 Since you're turning frontside, you'll need to apply some pressure with your heels on the edge of the board, just like if you were turning in the street.

5 Come out of your carve at a slight angle, and stand up straight as you hit the flat-bottom so that you're ready for the next wall.

It takes some time and practice to get carving down. You can pick up the basics in a day or two, but sometimes it takes a while before you really feel comfortable carving in a bowl. Be patient and persistent because you really need to have carving mastered before you move on to more advanced bowl tricks.

While you're learning, set some small goals for yourself. See how many corners you can carve in one run. Try working yourself up higher and higher toward the lip of the bowl. As you start to get the hang of it, try coming out of a backside carve in one corner and then hitting a frontside carve in another corner, a line known as a figure 8.

Carve Trains

Once you and some friends master the fine art of carving, you're ready to catch a carve train. Trains are best with about three people—any more and it'll be more like a crash-up derby than a train.

So here's how it goes: The first person drops in and starts to carve through the bowl, followed by the second person, who follows the first person's lines. And then the third person does the same until you have a little skate train going. It's fun to see how long you can keep everyone together.

Trains are also good because following a friend forces you to try new lines. Make sure to watch out for each other, and always let the fastest skater go first so he or she doesn't run over his or her slower buddies.

CHAPTER 3
Basic Bowl Tricks

Learning to skate a bowl is sort of like building a house—you need a solid foundation before you can move ahead. With bowl skating, that foundation is carving. So if you have the carve down, you're ready to start learning some basic tricks. If not, keep working at it and you'll get it soon enough.

The tricks in this book are divided into three categories: basic, intermediate, and advanced. Basic tricks are the easiest to learn, and like the rough framework built on top of a foundation, you need to start out with these before you add anything else. We also recommend you learn most of the following tricks on a regular half-pipe before you attempt them in a bowl.

Backside Grind

Grinds are some of the most common and fun bowl tricks. A grind is a trick where one or both of your trucks makes contact with and slides, or grinds, along the coping.

There are all kinds of different grinds you can do, but first you need to get the basic grind down. If you can already do this on a regular half-pipe, it comes pretty naturally in a bowl. And remember how we told you to keep four on the floor when carving? When learning basic grinds in a bowl, it's OK to lift your front trucks and wheels off the surface, just like you would for a grind in a half-pipe. Try your first grinds in a shallow section of the pool, working your way into the deeper sections.

BACKSIDE GRIND

 Approach the corner with enough speed to reach the lip of the bowl.

As you begin your carve, raise your back heel just a bit and use your back toes to put a little extra pressure on the edge of your tail, which will also lift your front trucks and wheels over the coping. This makes it easier for your back wheel to roll over the coping, so that your back truck can contact the lip.

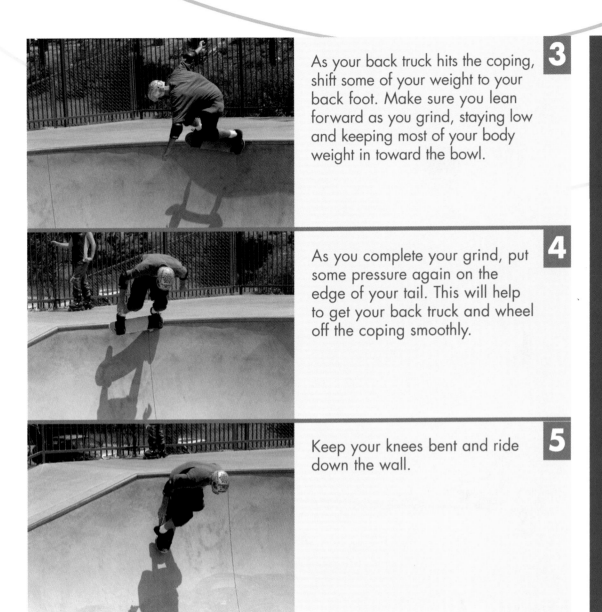

3 As your back truck hits the coping, shift some of your weight to your back foot. Make sure you lean forward as you grind, staying low and keeping most of your body weight in toward the bowl.

4 As you complete your grind, put some pressure again on the edge of your tail. This will help to get your back truck and wheel off the coping smoothly.

5 Keep your knees bent and ride down the wall.

Frontside Grind

Once you get the basic backside grind down, it's time to learn the frontside grind. Although they're both basic grinds and they involve some similar motions, they feel completely different when you do them.

FRONTSIDE GRIND

1 Carve into the corner with plenty of speed.

2 Use your toe and the ball of your foot to press down slightly on your tail.

3 Lift up your front trucks and wheels, and let your back truck grind on the coping. Shift most of your weight to your back foot and keep your knees bent as you grind.

4 As you complete your grind, begin to turn your hips and lead shoulder back into the bowl.

Look over your lead shoulder and ride back in.

Carve Grind

Once you get the hang of simple grinds (some people call them scratcher grinds because you're basically just scratching the coping), you can try a slightly more advanced trick called the carve grind.

Carve grinds involve a motion similar to basic grinds, except that instead of lifting your front trucks, you allow them to grind along with your back trucks. Carve grinds allow you to get more speed than a basic grind, and they'll also help you learn more advanced grinds like the 50-50. If you have basic carves down, they're really pretty simple.

Carve into the corner at a wider angle and with a little more speed than you would for a basic grind.

CARVE GRIND

(continued on page 26)

2 As you approach the lip, apply some pressure on the edge of your board with your toes and the balls of your feet. This will allow both your front and back trucks to contact the coping and grind.

3 As you lead up to your grind, lean forward and keep your whole body in toward the bowl.

4 As your grind begins to end, again apply a little pressure with your toes and the balls of your feet. This will help get your wheels and trucks off the coping so you can ride smoothly back into the bowl.

5 Once both your trucks are off the coping, carve back down the wall and ride into the flat-bottom.

Axle Stall

Axle stalls are another important foundation trick that will eventually help you learn 50-50s in a bowl. They're also a good setup trick, which means they're the kind of basic trick that allow you to rest just for a second and prepare for harder tricks. To do an axle stall, you set both trucks square on the coping and stall for a moment. Here's how it's done:

1 Unlike a grind, for an axle stall you want to avoid carving and instead make more of a straight-line approach to the lip. You also need some extra speed to get all the way on top of the deck, but not so much that you overshoot the coping.

2 As you reach the top of the bowl, press down on your tail and lift up your front trucks so that they don't hit the coping.

3 Set your back truck on the coping first, putting some extra weight on your back heel so you can get your board and body all the way up on the deck.

AXLE STALL

(continued on page 28)

4 Once your back truck is resting on the coping, use it as your pivot point, bringing your shoulders and hips around so they're parallel with the coping below you. Set your front trucks down, keeping the weight on your heels and your body leaning in toward the bowl.

5 After you stall for a second, press down on your tail with the toes of your back foot. Rotate your hips and shoulders, lean forward, and turn off the coping.

6 Ride back into the bowl.

Backside Rock-and-Rolls

The rock-and-roll is a classic beginner bowl trick. Like the axle stall, the rock-and-roll is a good setup trick, too.

Without carving, ride straight up the transition with enough speed to reach the lip.

As you approach the lip, press down on the tail with your back foot and use your front foot to lift your front trucks and wheels over the coping. As you do this, begin to rotate your torso and shoulder back toward the side so that they're almost parallel with the coping.

Set the center of your board down on the coping by using your foot to press your front truck and wheels down on the deck. At the same time, bend your back knee. These two motions combined will make your back wheels come off the ramp in a rocking (or teetering) motion.

While your board stalls briefly on the coping and the deck, keep leaning your body back into the transition and continue rotating your upper body backward. This will make it easier to reenter the bowl.

(continued on page 30)

5 As you begin to reenter, press down on your tail, shifting weight off your front foot. Continue rotating your body so that your shoulders and hips come all the way around and face the opposite side of the bowl.

6 Set your front trucks back down on the wall, keeping your knees bent as you roll down the tranny.

A more advanced version of the rock-and-roll is called the boardslide. It's the same basic trick, except that you actually slide across the coping on your board. To do a boardslide, approach the lip with more speed and at a sharper angle, which will give you the momentum to slide.

CHAPTER 4

Intermediate Bowl Tricks

So you have all the beginner tricks down, right? Then it's time to step it up to some harder tricks. Now that you're more comfortable with carving, you're probably skating a lot faster in the bowl. That's good, because you'll need the extra speed for this next round of tricks.

One trick that definitely takes a little more speed is the 50-50 grind. This is an essential bowl trick. The 50-50 helps you get speed for advanced tricks like airs and inverts. A 50-50 involves almost the same motions as an axle stall, except you actually grind across the coping instead of just stalling. Once you get 50-50s wired, try grinding though the entire corner.

50-50 Grind

If you have axle stalls and carve grinds down, 50-50s will come naturally to you.

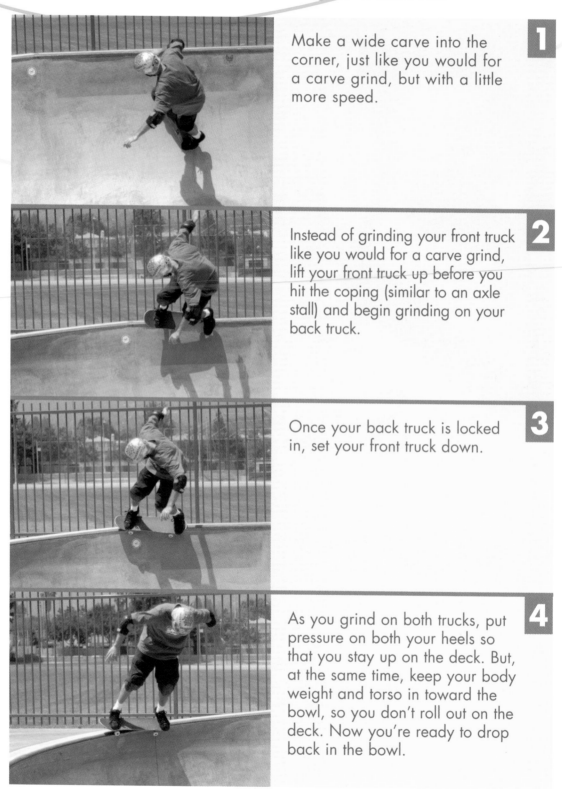

1 Make a wide carve into the corner, just like you would for a carve grind, but with a little more speed.

2 Instead of grinding your front truck like you would for a carve grind, lift your front truck up before you hit the coping (similar to an axle stall) and begin grinding on your back truck.

3 Once your back truck is locked in, set your front truck down.

4 As you grind on both trucks, put pressure on both your heels so that you stay up on the deck. But, at the same time, keep your body weight and torso in toward the bowl, so you don't roll out on the deck. Now you're ready to drop back in the bowl.

5 If your trucks are locked into the coping, they'll naturally guide you through the bowl's curved shape. But you can use your toes and the balls of your feet to make slight corrections.

6 As you complete your grind, press down on your tail with the ball of your back foot while turning your hips and shoulders back into the bowl.

7 Keep your knees bent slightly. As you drop back in, head toward the opposite wall.

Frontside 5-0

The 5-0 is also sometimes called a stand-up grind because, unlike the basic frontside grind, you actually stand all the way up on the coping as you grind. If you have trouble standing up on your grinds in a bowl with concrete coping, you might have to do a small floating hop to get on the coping. Also, some people consider it cheating, but it sometimes helps to drag your back heel on the coping while you learn this trick.

FRONTSIDE 5-0

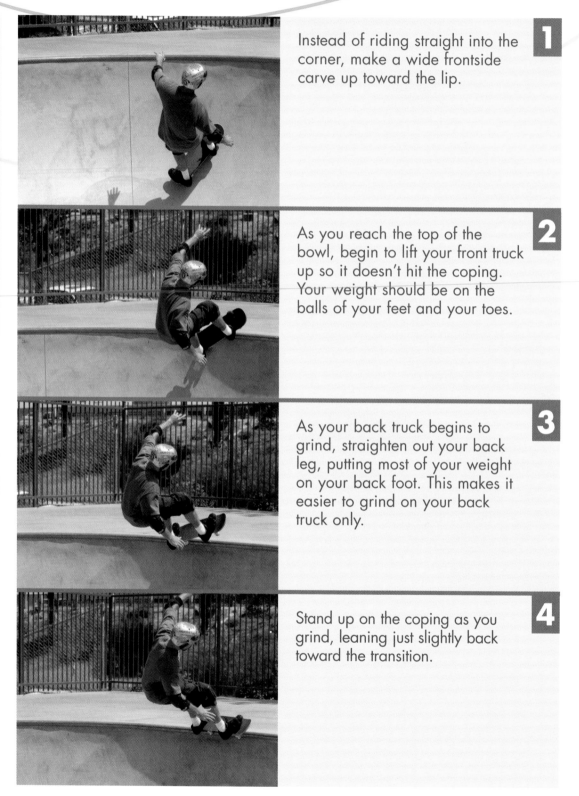

1 Instead of riding straight into the corner, make a wide frontside carve up toward the lip.

2 As you reach the top of the bowl, begin to lift your front truck up so it doesn't hit the coping. Your weight should be on the balls of your feet and your toes.

3 As your back truck begins to grind, straighten out your back leg, putting most of your weight on your back foot. This makes it easier to grind on your back truck only.

4 Stand up on the coping as you grind, leaning just slightly back toward the transition.

5 As your grind ends, put some pressure on your tail and start guiding your board back into the bowl.

6 Use your front foot to press down on the board so that your front truck and wheels touch back down on the bowl surface.

7 Bend your knees slightly as you roll back in.

Frontside Layback Grind to Tail

The layback grind, like the rock-and-roll, is another classic old-school trick. ("Old school" is a term used to describe tricks that have been around for decades.) To do this trick, you need to have the frontside 50-50 down.

35

FRONTSIDE LAYBACK GRIND TO TAIL

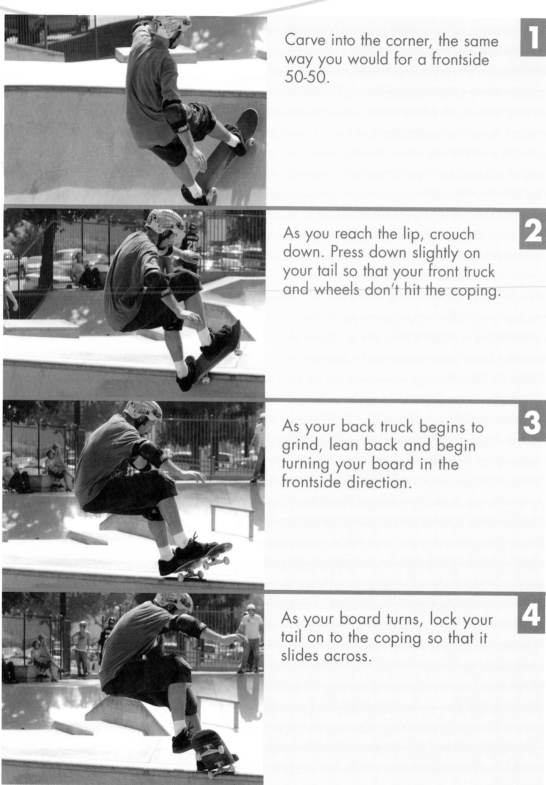

1 Carve into the corner, the same way you would for a frontside 50-50.

2 As you reach the lip, crouch down. Press down slightly on your tail so that your front truck and wheels don't hit the coping.

3 As your back truck begins to grind, lean back and begin turning your board in the frontside direction.

4 As your board turns, lock your tail on to the coping so that it slides across.

5 As you finish your grind, place your back hand on the coping for support and push your way across the lip.

6 Push off the coping with your back hand to help you stand up and roll back into the bowl.

Layback grinds can also be done backside. It's pretty much the same motion, except most skaters grab the nose of the board when they do this trick backside.

CHAPTER 5
Advanced Bowl Tricks

Now that you have some intermediate tricks under your belt, you're ready for the most difficult bowl tricks.

Frontside Smith Grind

Smiths are one of the trickiest grinds, and you should definitely have frontside 5-0s on lockdown before you try them. A smith is a grind where your back truck is on the coping and your front truck is below the coping, so that you're actually sliding on the bottom of your board at the same time you grind.

Smith grinds are both stylish and challenging. They look good but require good balance and precision. Since the board is grinding at an angle, its natural tendency is to push off the coping. The key is to maintain your balance while looking graceful. The following sequence will show you how to do them.

 Carve frontside into the bowl, the same way you would for a frontside 5-0.

 Press down on your tail to lift up your front trucks and wheels as you approach the coping.

 Lean back and bend your back knee as you begin to grind with your back truck. Once you're all the way on the coping, straighten out your front leg, point your toes, and push your nose down below the coping.

 As you grind, keep your weight on your back truck, which will keep you locked into the smith position.

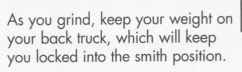

(Continued on page 40)

FRONTSIDE SMITH GRIND

Frontside Smith Grind *(continued)*

5 Once you complete your grind, press down on your tail with your heel to get your back truck off the coping. Begin to turn your shoulders and hips back into the ramp.

6 Bend your knees slightly as you roll back into the bowl and prepare for your next trick.

Frontside Air over a Hip

In order to do airs over a hip, it helps to be comfortable doing regular frontside airs on a half-pipe, which is described in *Rippin' Ramps: The Skateboarder's Guide to Riding Half-Pipes.*

However, some people find that hip airs are actually easier than regular airs. And different people have different ways of doing hip airs. Some skaters snap their tail and pop an ollie before grabbing the board. Others simply bounce (or, as most people call it, bonk) their wheels on the coping and then let their momentum boost them into the air, without hitting their tail. We recommend you try the non-ollie method first, and then if you want more height, you can learn to pop into the trick.

1 Approach the hip at a slight angle. Your weight should be on the balls of your feet and your toes.

2 Press down on your tail a bit as you reach the coping in order to lift your front trucks over and bonk your wheels off the coping.

3 As you launch in the air, lean back and tuck your knees up toward your body, lifting your board high enough for you to grab. Reach down with your back hand and let the board float up into your grip. Once you grab, pull up on the board and slightly tuck your body.

4 Getting in the air is pretty easy. It's landing that's tricky. So here's the secret: when you're up in the air, look down and spot the exact point on the wall where you'll land.

FRONTSIDE AIR OVER A HIP

(continued on page 42)

5 Let go of the board before setting it down, and keep your knees bent slightly as you ride smoothly down the other side of the hip.

Backside Air

To do a backside air, you launch out of the bowl backside and grab the board with your lead hand. It's a pretty tough one to pull off in a bowl. This is one trick that's actually easier to learn in a steeper, larger bowl because the vert actually launches you up in the air.

BACKSIDE AIR

1 Approach the lip backside with tons of speed as you reach down toward the board with your lead hand.

2 Press down on your tail as you approach the coping. Let your back wheels bonk off the coping and lean into the bowl while grabbing the board.

3 Keep your body tucked and leaning forward as you reach the peak of your air.

4 Before you start to come down, spot the point on the transition where you'll land.

5 Let go of the board as you start to come down. Be careful not to get your back wheels caught on the coping as you land.

6 Set the board down and roll down the wall.

GLOSSARY

backside Any trick in which you turn in the direction of your toes.

bail Another name for falling off your skateboard. A hard fall is usually called a slam.

carving A method of riding through a bowl or pool in a way that increases your speed.

frontside Any trick in which you turn in the direction of your heels.

line Linking together a whole series of different tricks, rather than just doing a single trick, while utilizing many of the bowl's features.

lockdown A term used to describe a trick that a skater can land almost every time.

rip To skate with a lot of skill, style, speed, and consistency.

session A meeting where two or more skaters get together and skate.

skate key A small tool used for tightening or loosening the trucks of a skateboard.

tail The rear part of the skateboard that angles upward.

truck The metal device that holds the wheels of a skateboard to the deck that makes it possible to turn.

wired The same as "lockdown"; it is a term used to describe a trick that is mastered.

Skateboardpark.com
1927 Harbor Boulevard, Suite 611
Costa Mesa, CA 92627
Web site: http://www.skateboardpark.com

Skatelab Indoor Skatepark and Museum
4226 Valley Fair Street
Simi Valley, CA 93063
(805) 578-0040
e-mail: info@skatelab.com
Web site: http://www.skatelab.com

Skatepark of Tampa
4215 East Columbus Drive
Tampa, FL 33605
(813) 621-6793
e-mail: info@skateparkoftampa.com
Web site: http://www.skateparkoftampa.com

Web Sites

Due to the changing nature of Internet links, the Rosen Publishing Group, Inc. has developed an online list of Web sites related to the subject of this book. This site is updated regularly. Please use this link to access the list:

http://www.rosenlinks.com/skgu/ofwa

FOR FURTHER READING

Brooke, Michael. *The Concrete Wave: The History of Skateboarding.* Toronto: Warwick Publishing, 1999.

Davis, Garry, and Craig Steycyk. *Dysfunctional.* Corte Madera, CA: Ginkgo Press, 1999.

Hawk, Tony. *Hawk: Occupation: Skateboarder.* New York: Regan Books, 2000.

Thatcher, Kevin. *Thrasher Presents How to Build Skateboard Ramps: Half-Pipes, Boxes, Bowls and More.* San Francisco: High Speed Productions, 2001.

Thrasher Magazine. *Thrasher: Insane Terrain.* New York: Universe Publishing, 2001.

Weyland, Jocko. *The Answer Is Never.* New York: Grove Press, 2002.

BIBLIOGRAPHY

Skateboardpark.com. "Iowa City Skatepark." Retrieved May 14, 2004 (http://www.skateboardpark.com/skateboardpark/viewpark.asp?ID=471).

Skateboardparks.com. "Verified Skateboard Parks." Retrieved March 2, 2004 (http://www.skateboardparks.com/verified.html).

Skatecity.com. "Where to Skate: Skateparks." Retrieved February 22, 2004 (http://www.skatecity.com/nyc/where/parks.html#pier26).

INDEX

About the Author

Justin Hocking lives and skateboards in New York City. He is also an editor of the book *Life and Limb: Skateboarders Write from the Deep End*, published in 2004 by Soft Skull Press.

Credits

All photos © Tony Donaldson/Icon SMI/The Rosen Publishing Group, except p. 4 © Peter Poby/Corbis.

Designer: Les Kanturek; Editor: Nicholas Croce;
Photo Research: Fernanda Rocha